D0349341

Dentist

Written by Deborah Chancellor
Photography by Chris Fairclough

W

FRANKLIN WATTS
LONDON • SYDNEY

First published in 2005 by Franklin Watts
96 Leonard Street, London EC2A 4XD

Franklin Watts Australia
45-51 Huntley Street, Alexandria, NSW 2015

© Franklin Watts 2005

Editors: Caryn Jenner, Sarah Ridley
Designer: Jemima Lumley
Art direction: Jonathan Hair
Photography: Chris Fairclough

The publisher wishes to thank Soula, Stratos, Nicholas, Angela,
Thomas and all the staff at Broxbourne Dental Care for their
assistance with the book.

Acknowledgement: photograph pg 28 (top) Ray Moller.

A CIP catalogue record for this book is available from the British
Library

ISBN 0 7496 6057 0

Dewey decimal classification number: 617.6

Printed in China

Contents

I am a dentist

My name is Soula.
I work at a dental
surgery.

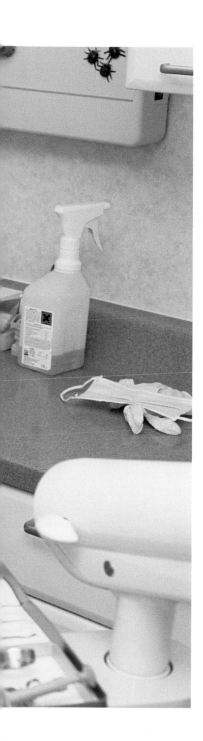

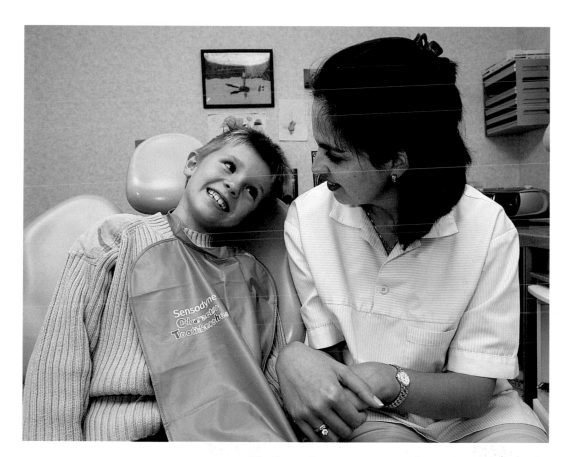

I help people to look
after their teeth.

Getting ready

Every morning, the receptionist gives me a list of my patients for the day.

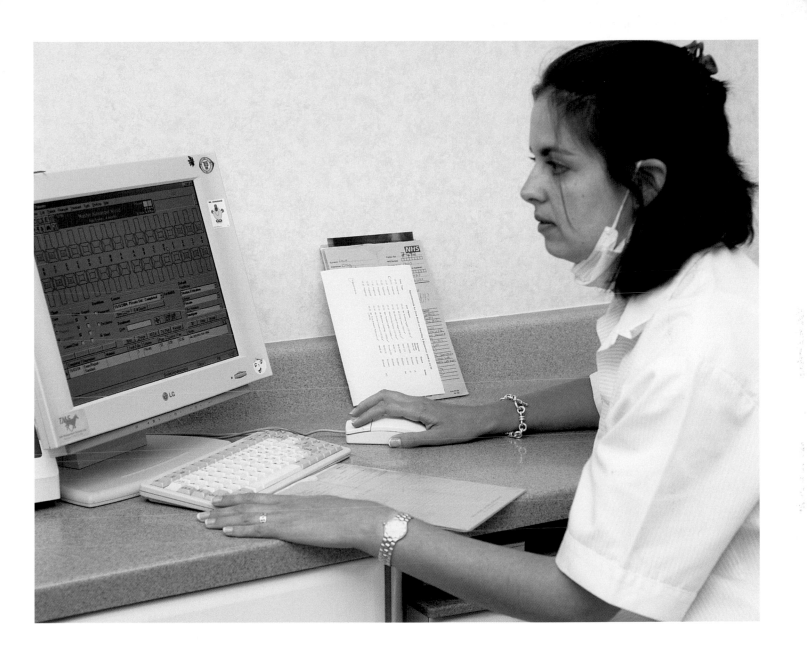

Before the surgery opens, I look at
the notes about each patient.

The dental nurse

My dental nurse is called Clare.
She tells patients when it is time
for their appointment.

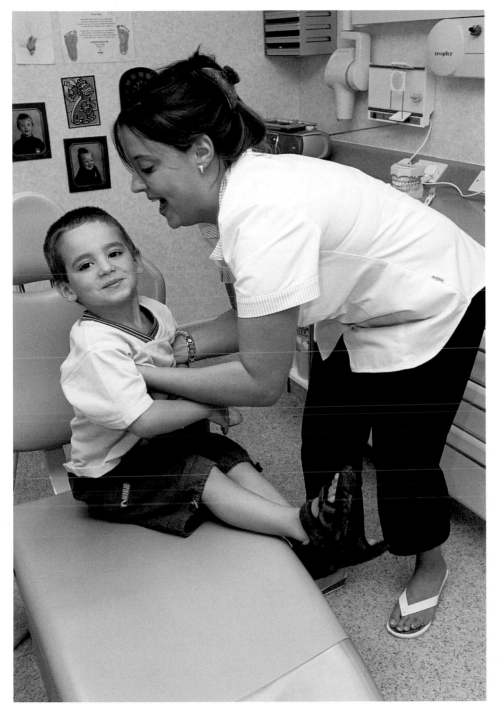

Clare helps Nicholas into the dentist's chair. He has come for a check-up.

Giving a check-up

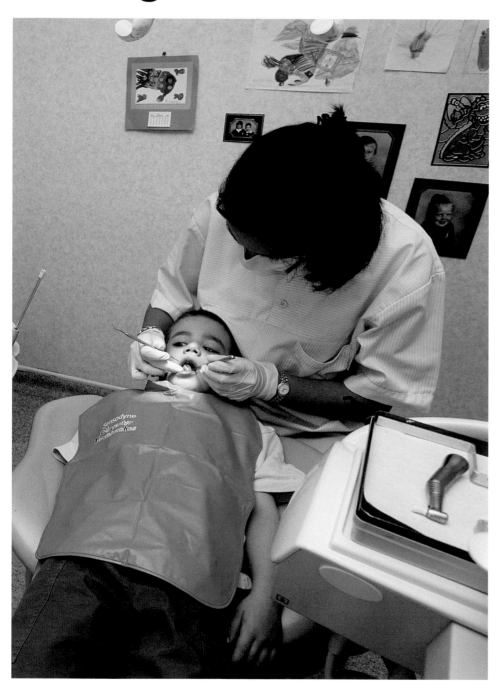

Nicholas opens his mouth wide. I use a small mirror to help me see all his teeth.

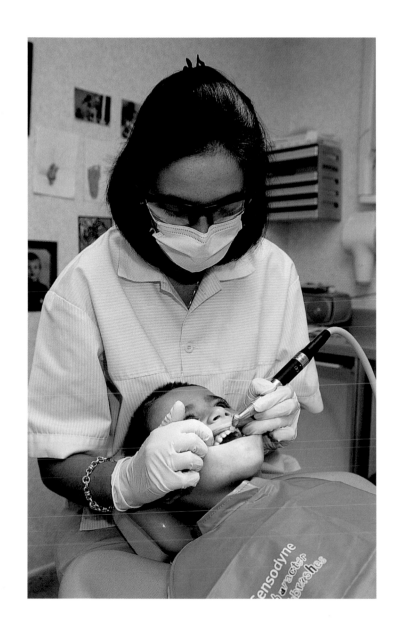

I clean Nicholas's teeth with polishing paste. Then he washes his mouth out with water.

After a check-up

Sometimes, I show patients how to clean their teeth at home. Look at my big toothbrush!

Nicholas has been very good.
I give him a sticker to say 'well done'.

A new patient

Keeley is visiting the surgery for the first time. She fills in a form at the reception desk.

At Keeley's first check-up,
we talk about her teeth.

Taking an X-ray

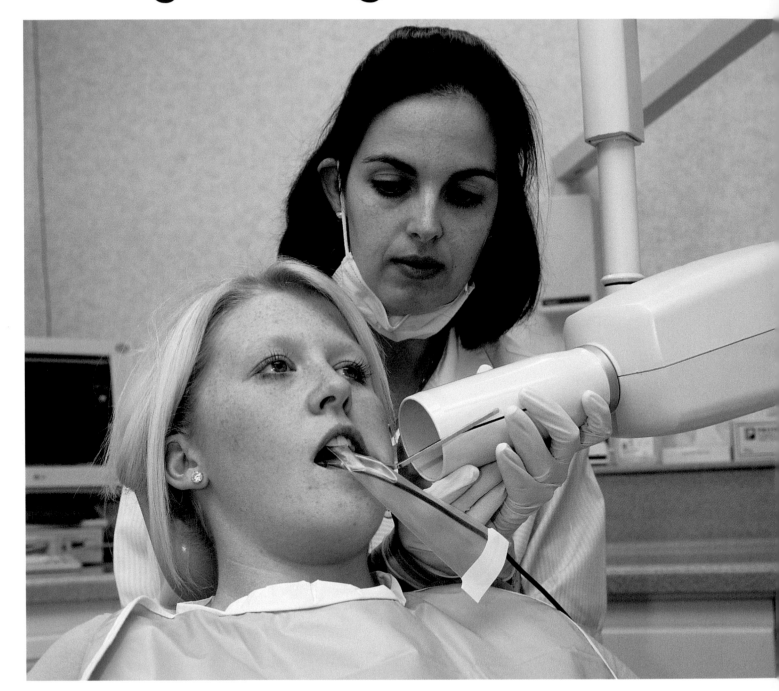

I take an X-ray of Keeley's teeth.

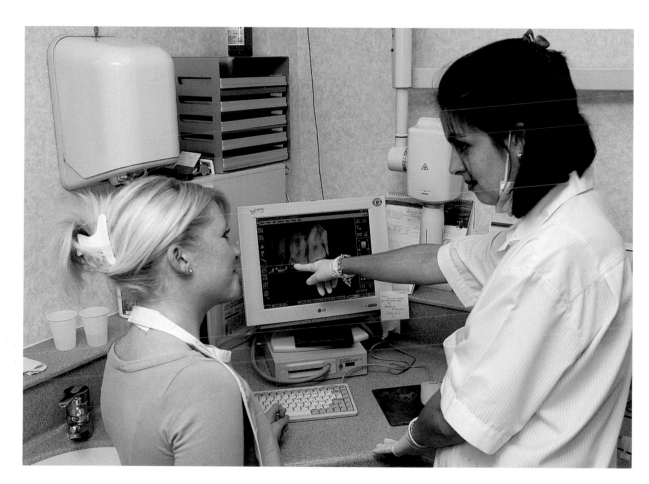

One of Keeley's teeth has a hole in it.
She will need a filling.

Filling a tooth

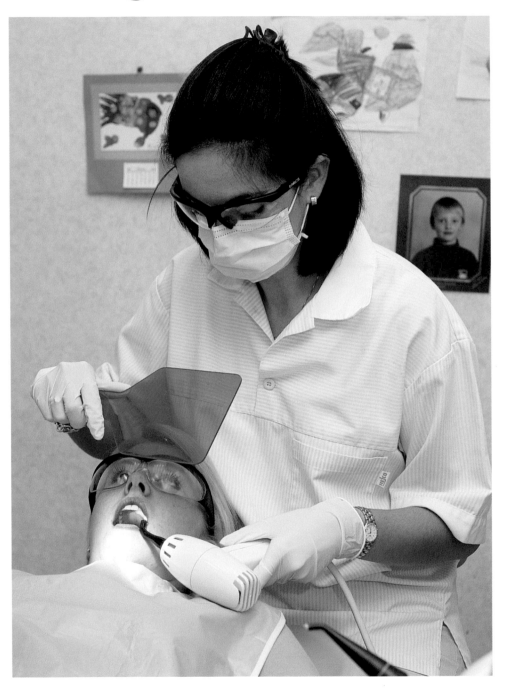

When I give Keeley her filling, we both wear goggles. This protects our eyes.

Afterwards Clare, the dental nurse, cleans my tools in a machine called a steriliser.

Emergency!

Sometimes I see emergency patients, like Thomas. He fell off his bike and knocked out a front tooth.

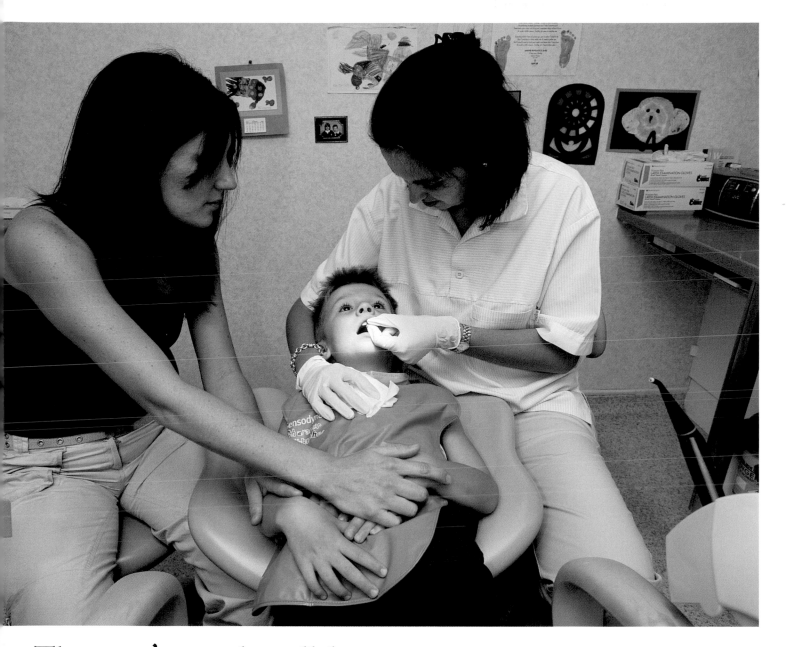

Thomas's tooth still has its root,
so I put it back into his gum.

Caring for teeth

When I see Thomas two months later, his tooth has grown back.

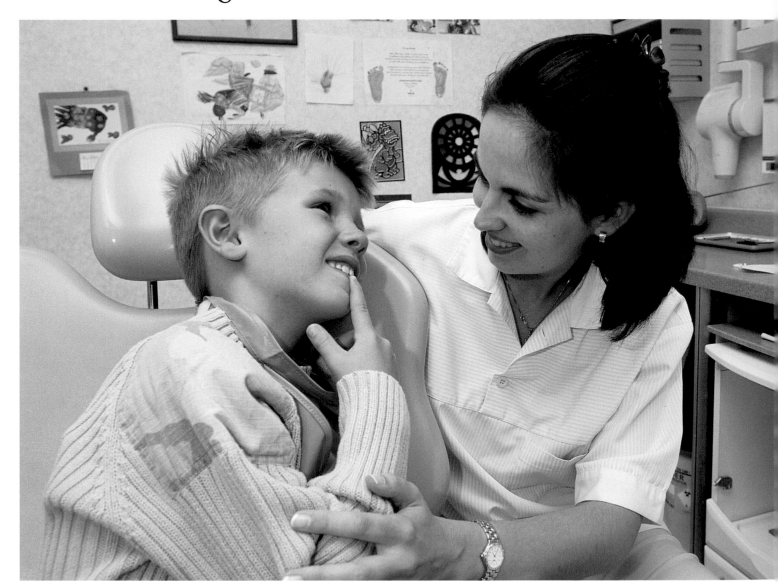

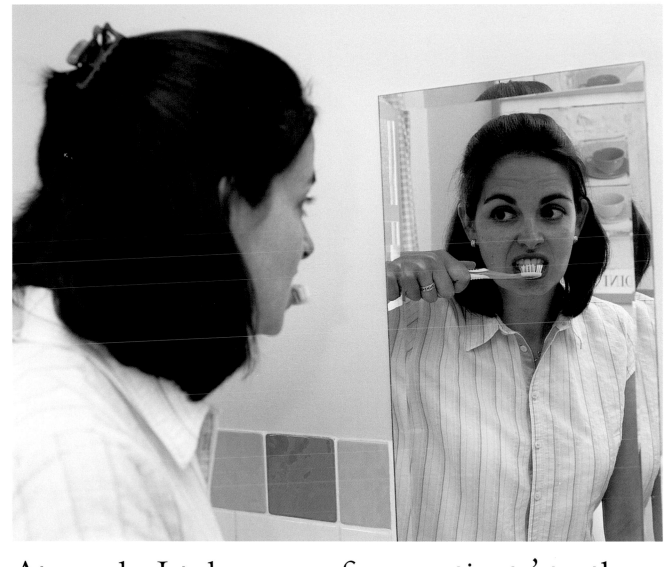

At work, I take care of my patients' teeth.
At home, I look after my own!

A dentist's equipment

Goggles protect the eyes of the dentist or patient.

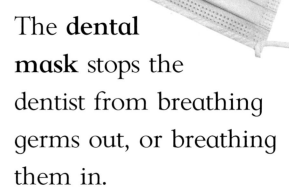

The **dental mask** stops the dentist from breathing germs out, or breathing them in.

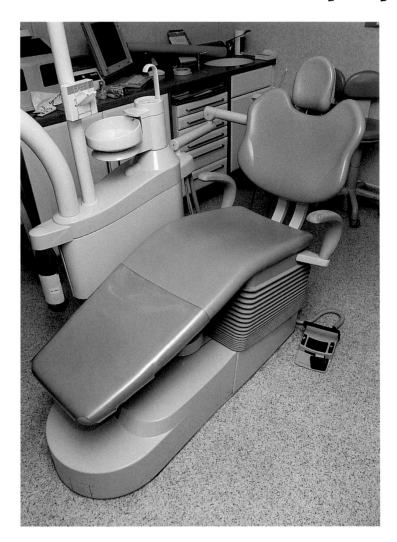

The **dentist's chair** lifts up and down and tilts forwards and backwards.

The dentist puts on new, clean **gloves** for each patient.

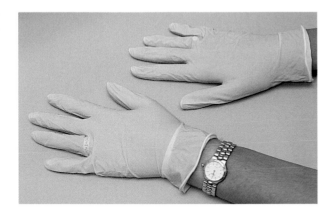

The **X-ray machine** takes pictures which show dentists what is happening inside teeth and gums.

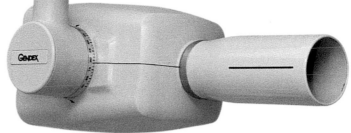

The dentist uses special **tools** to look after a patient's teeth.

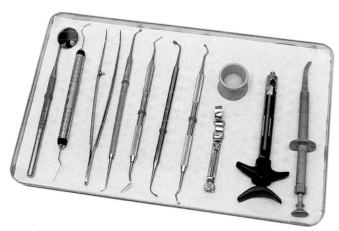

After treatment, patients wash their mouths out with flavoured **water**.

Your teeth

You have 20 milk teeth. When you are five or six years old, your milk teeth start to fall out.

This makes space for bigger teeth to grow. Look after your second set of teeth very carefully. These teeth must last your whole life!

- Remember to clean your teeth every morning and evening.
- Use a small blob of toothpaste on your toothbrush.
- Ask for a new toothbrush when your old one is worn out. Bent bristles don't clean teeth very well!

Glossary and index